Creative Keyboard Presents

instant recital

LEVEL ONE

By Uri Ayn Rovner

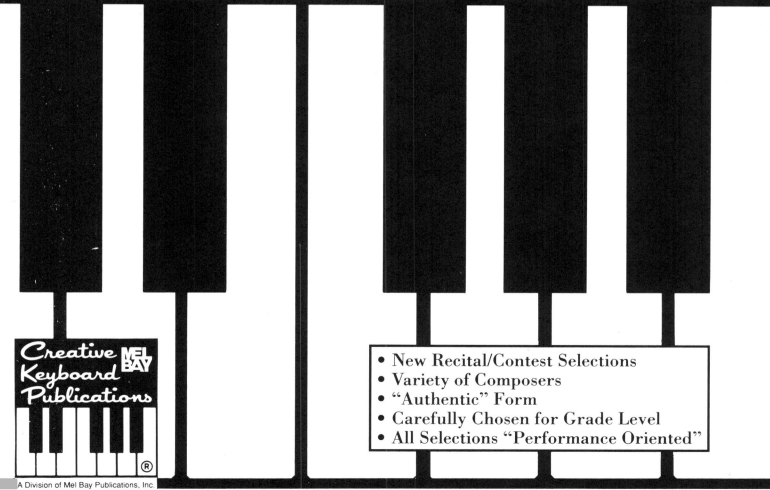

Creative Keyboard Publications
MEL BAY
A Division of Mel Bay Publications, Inc.

- New Recital/Contest Selections
- Variety of Composers
- "Authentic" Form
- Carefully Chosen for Grade Level
- All Selections "Performance Oriented"

FOREWORD

In the "Instant Recital" Series, students have a variety of shorter works that have been carefully chosen or written for performance in recitals or contests. They are fun to play and fun to hear. The selections are in authentic form so that each may be used for audition or to demonstrate achievement.

Each volume spans hundreds of years of piano composition by those composers who taught piano and wrote specifically for their students.

Use the "Instant Recital" Series as a supplement to any method book or music program, and open the doors to happy performing!

TO THE TEACHER

Selecting the correct piano pieces for a beginner to perform can be tricky. This volume offers a variety of pieces, many of which are less often heard, of different lengths. These selections are not meant to be used in any particular order. Enjoy them however best fits your student.

In choosing these pieces, hand shapes and required dexterity for the beginner were always considered. Care was taken to avoid pieces with sustained octaves in either hand. Fingerings are *guidelines*. When needed, change the fingerings to help your student play with more comfort or accuracy.

This book was composed by piano teachers who made student performance a priority. They would be happy to know we still use them!

CONTENTS

1. D. G. Türk
Nieten? Nieten? 7
Happy Hans 8

2. A. Reinagle
Minuetto 9

3. J. G. Schetky
Air 10

4. C. Czerny
Hopping on One Foot 12
Stück 14
Austrian Waltz 15

5. F. Schubert
Ländler 16

6. F. Spindler
Canon 17

7. L. Schytte
Sailor's Song 18

8. D. B. Kabalevsky
Polka 19
A Little Dance 20

9. U. A. Rovner
On Dit 21
En Vacances 22

NIETEN? NIETEN?

Moderato

D. G. TÜRK

HAPPY HANS

Allegro moderato

D. G. TÜRK

MINUETTO

Allegretto

A. REINAGLE

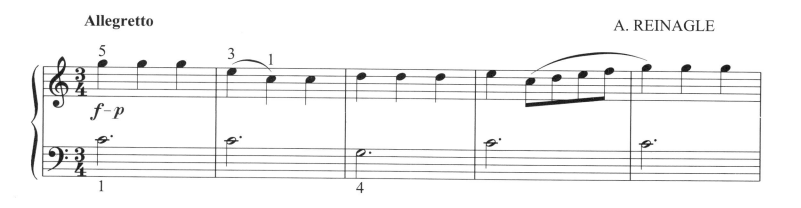

J. GEORGE SCHETKY (1776–1831)
This Scottish-born American was the son of a composer and cellist. Some of his music was published in *Carr's Music Journal* in Philadelphia, where he taught and performed.

AIR

JOHN GEORGE SCHETKY

CARL CZERNY (1791–1857)
Czerny's father helped him work on pieces by Bach, Mozart, and Clementi. Soon he was studying with Beethoven, all of whose piano works Czerny could perform by memory. There are many hundreds of short pieces like these among his compositions.

HOPPING ON ONE FOOT

Allegretto

C. CZERNY

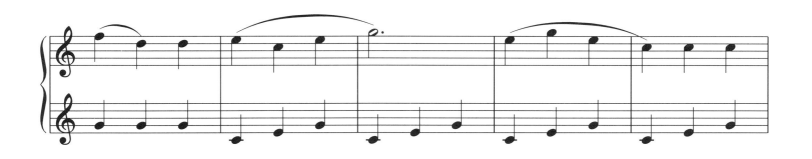

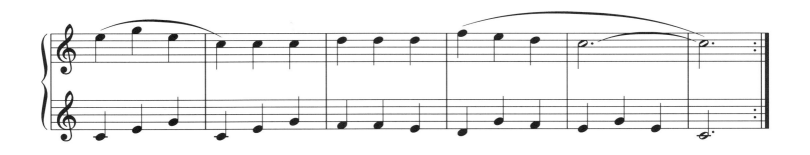

STÜCK

Moderato

C. CZERNY

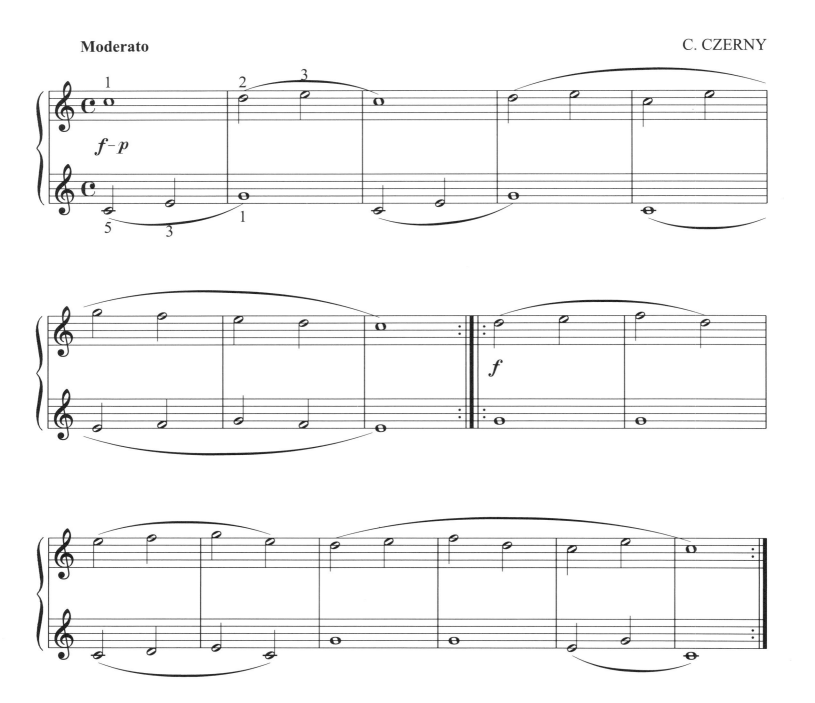

AUSTRIAN WALTZ

LÄNDLER

FRANZ SCHUBERT

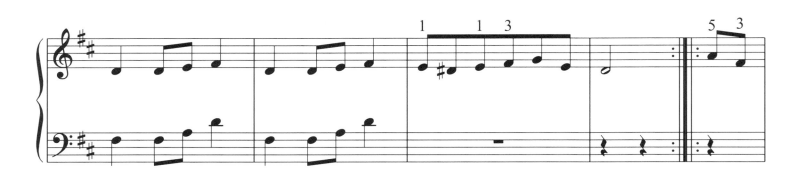

FRITZ SPINDLER (1817–1905)

Fritz Spindler was a German pianist and composer who wrote mostly piano teaching pieces. A canon is a round which is played rather than sung. You may try playing this one twice through, the second time an octave higher.

CANON

F. SPINDLER

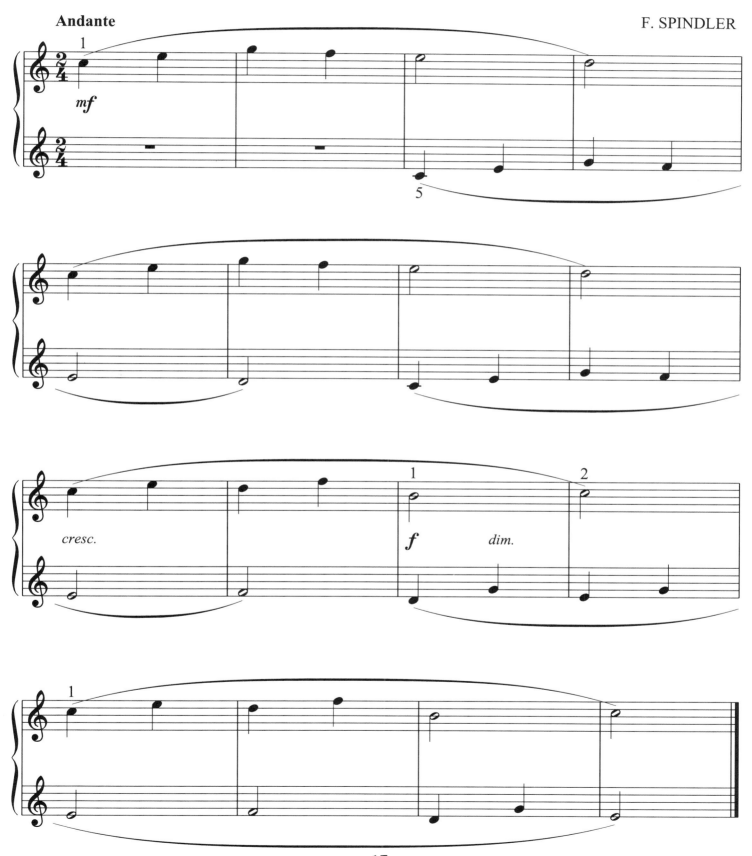

LUDVIG SCHYTTE (1848–1909)

This Danish composer and pianist was originally a chemist and had no music education until he was 22. Then he began to study the piano and was soon teaching music in Vienna and Berlin. He wrote many lesson books with etudes like "Sailor's Song."

SAILOR'S SONG

L. SCHYTTE

DMITRI BORISOVICH KABALEVSKY (1904–1987)

As a young boy in Russia, Dmitri played piano by ear. He grew to be a composer of opera, ballet, and music for silent film. He was also a poet and artist. These two selections come from *24 Pieces For Children*.

POLKA

D. KABALEVSKY

A LITTLE DANCE

Allegro Molto

D. KABALEVSKY

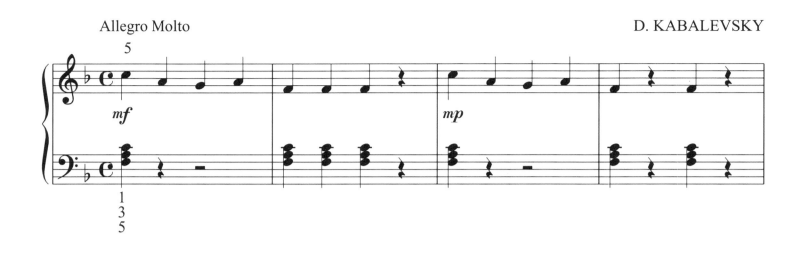

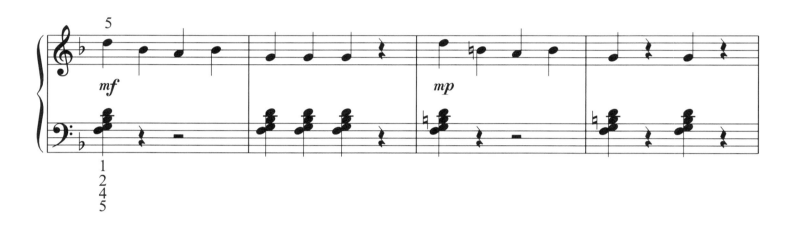

URI AYN ROVNER (1951–)

Uri Ayn Rovner, a teacher and performer in Colorado, enjoys writing songs for piano students. In New England when he was young, Rovner loved driving trips to the ocean. In "En Vacances," choose your own tempo to create the excitement of going "on vacation." "On Dit" ("One Says") is played on the black keys only.

ON DIT

U. A. ROVNER

EN VACANCES

U. A. ROVNER

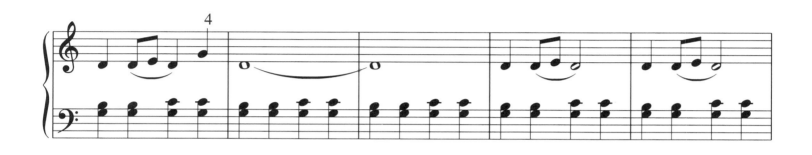

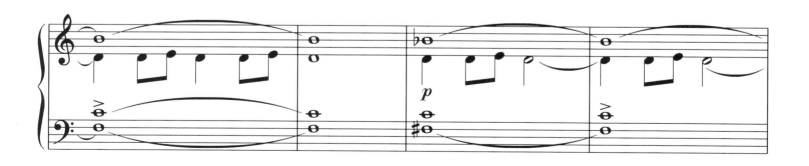

D. S. al $\oplus$

$\oplus$ CODA

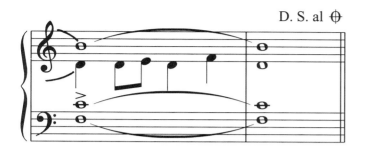